you can draw anything

kim gamble

DAZZLE THE DOG! SHOCK THE CHOOK! AMAZE YOUR FRIENDS!

YOU CAN DRAW!

ANYTHING! DRAWING IS NOT DIFFICULT!
YOU LOOK, YOU SEE, AND YOU DRAW WHAT YOU SEE! SEE?

YOU DO, HOWEVER, NEED TO KNOW HOW TO **SEE.**
WHEN YOU LOOK AT WHAT YOU WANT TO DRAW, LOOK FOR THE **SIMPLE** SHAPES AND LINES. DON'T WORRY ABOUT DETAILS, JUST LOOK FOR THE SIMPLEST SHAPES AND LINES, AND DRAW THEM.

ALL THE SHAPES AND LINES YOU'LL NEED ARE ONES YOU **ALREADY** KNOW HOW TO DRAW – THEY'RE THE LETTERS OF THE **ALPHABET**, AND **NUMBERS**!

A TIGER, FOR EXAMPLE, MIGHT BE S, O, C, V, a, 5, AND SO ON, BUT YOU HAVE TO BE ABLE TO **SEE** THESE LINES.

Is your pencil sharp? Let's begin!

Decide which way around to put your paper.

Hold the pencil lightly, relax.

IMAGINE EACH LINE, ON THE PAPER, BEFORE YOU DRAW IT.

Imagine it from beginning to end.

SEE where it will go, and draw it there.

Draw lightly and don't worry about mistakes. Draw over them, use them to guide you. Erase mistakes later if you don't like them.

Start with **A JOCOSAURUS**. All you'll need are the letters of its name.

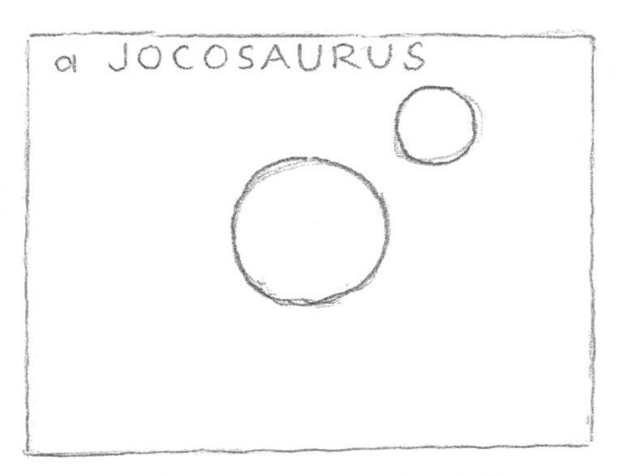

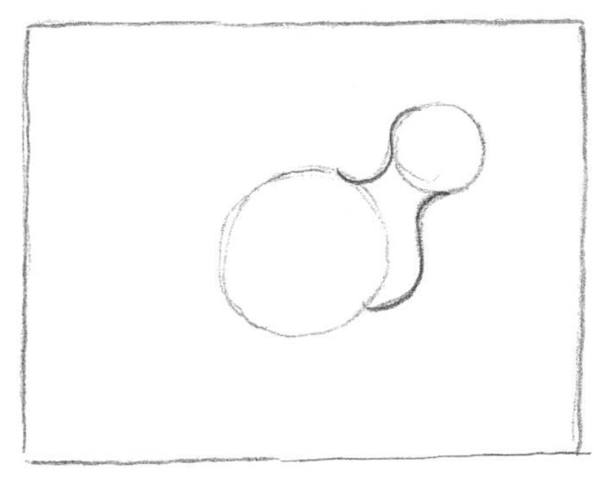

① Begin with the Os.

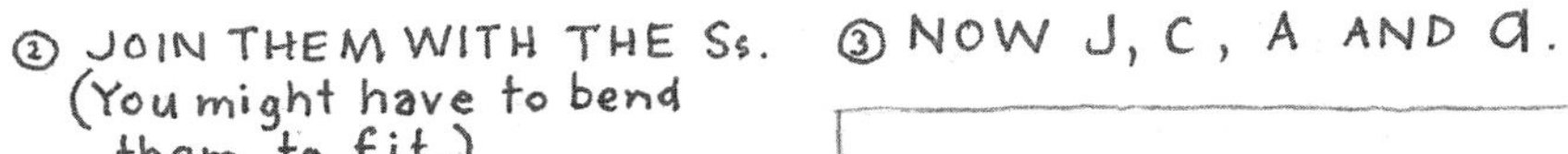

② Join them with the Ss. (You might have to bend them to fit.)

③ Now J, C, A and a.

④ Now the R and Us.

If you think this is looking more like an angry duck than a dinosaur, remember – they **ARE** related.

⑤ ... just thicken the tail and legs, add a nose, teeth and front legs, and ...

IF YOUR JOCOSAURUS DIDN'T TURN OUT THE WAY YOU WANTED IT TO, PERHAPS THE PROBLEM BEGAN WITH YOUR **O**s. ARE THEY **ROUND**? ARE THEY THE RIGHT **SIZE**? ARE THEY IN THE RIGHT **POSITION**?

TRY THIS:

① BEGIN WITH A CIRCLE. LET YOUR HAND **GLIDE**, AROUND AND AROUND, YOUR LITTLE FINGER JUST BRUSHING THE PAPER.

DRAW LIGHTLY. DON'T STOP TO RUB OUT.

② LIGHTLY DIVIDE YOUR CIRCLE THROUGH THE CENTRE, DOWN AND ACROSS.

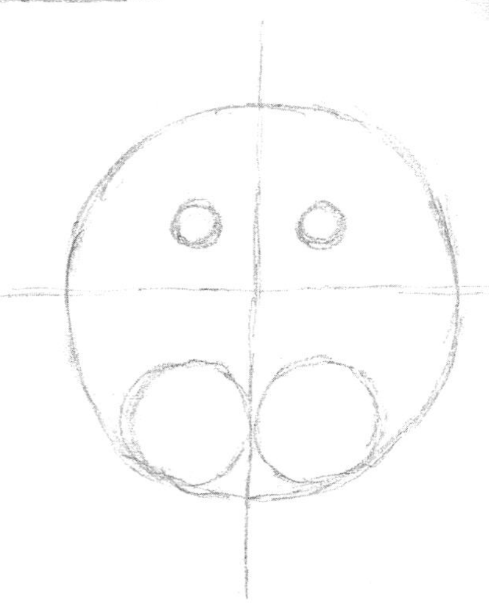

③ MAKE 2 SMALL CIRCLES IN EACH TOP SECTION, AND 2 LARGER CIRCLES BELOW.

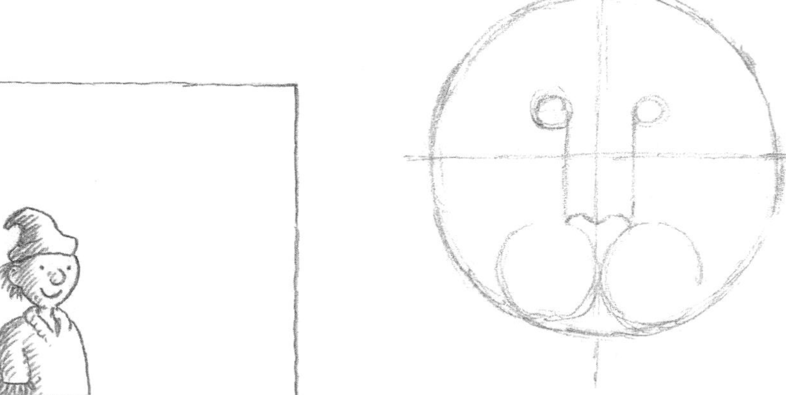

④ DRAW 2 LINES FROM THE INSIDE OF THE TOP CIRCLES TO THE ONES BELOW, AND JOIN THEM WITH A ◡◡ LINE.

⑤ MAKE 3 HALF-CIRCLES, OR C-SHAPES, FOR EARS AND A CHIN.

⑥ MAKE SHORT, LIGHT DASHES FOR A NECK MANE.

⑦ SHORTER WHISKERS FOR THE CHIN AND EARS, LONG CURVES FOR THE CHEEK WHISKERS.

⑧ ADD EYEBALLS AND TEETH, AND DRAW IN THE STRIPES LIGHTLY.

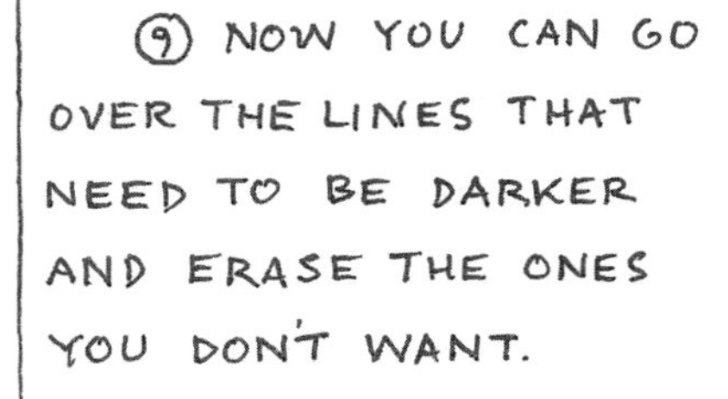

⑨ NOW YOU CAN GO OVER THE LINES THAT NEED TO BE DARKER AND ERASE THE ONES YOU DON'T WANT.

IF YOUR TIGER LOOKED LIKE THIS, MAYBE YOU NEED A LITTLE MORE **CIRCLE** PRACTICE.

TAKE A SHEET OF PAPER, AND DRAW A BIG CIRCLE, AROUND AND AROUND, MOVING YOUR HAND, YOUR WRIST, EVEN YOUR **ARM** IF YOU HAVE ROOM!

MAKE LOTS OF CIRCLES AND MAKE THEM **ROUND**! MAKE SOME WITH SHORT, LIGHT STROKES – **EXPLORE** YOUR WAY AROUND!

MAYBE YOUR CIRCLES **ARE** ROUND, BUT YOU CAN'T MAKE THEM THE **SIZE** YOU WANT, OR YOU CAN'T DRAW THEM IN THE **POSITION** YOU WANT.
IT COMES BACK TO BEING ABLE TO **SEE**.

Take a quick look at this picture – what do you see?

3 columns and a roof? Look again.

See where the lines join, and how they help to make us see something which isn't there at all.

Even when something is right there in front of you, it's sometimes difficult to see it.

And if you can't **see** it, how can you **draw** it?

Once there were six very silly men who never opened their eyes.

"Why should we?" they said, "Our hands tell us all we need to know!"

One day, however, they found something new.

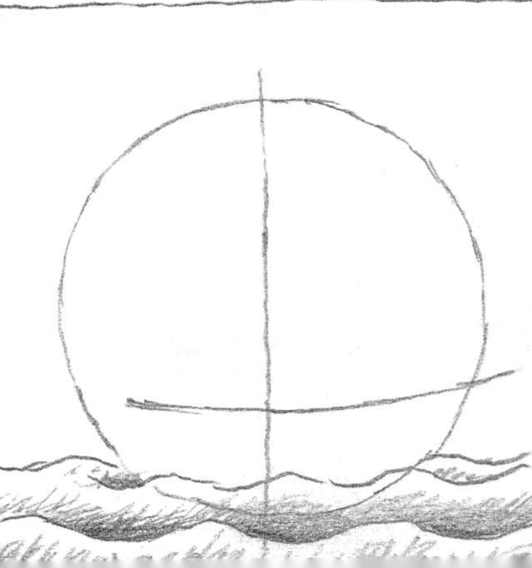

WHAT THE SIX SILLY MEN HAD FOUND, OF COURSE, WAS AN ELEPHANT!

IN ORDER TO DRAW, WE MUST OPEN OUR EYES AND SEE THE WHOLE PICTURE – THE **OVERALL SHAPE**.

THE OVERALL SHAPE OF THIS ELEPHANT IS A **RECTANGLE**.

① BEGIN THE ELEPHANT WITH A RECTANGLE.

② LOOK AT THE LINES THAT MAKE THE BOTTOM, THE FOREHEAD, AND THE SHAPE BETWEEN THE LEGS. DRAW THEM IN.

③ NOW DRAW THE J-SHAPES OF THE FRONT LEG, THE OTHER BACK LEG, AND THE TRUNK.

MAKE AN EAR WITH A C, AND AN EYE WITH A DOT.

④ FINISH WITH 2 CURVES FOR A TUSK, LITTLE Us FOR TOENAILS, AND A TAIL.

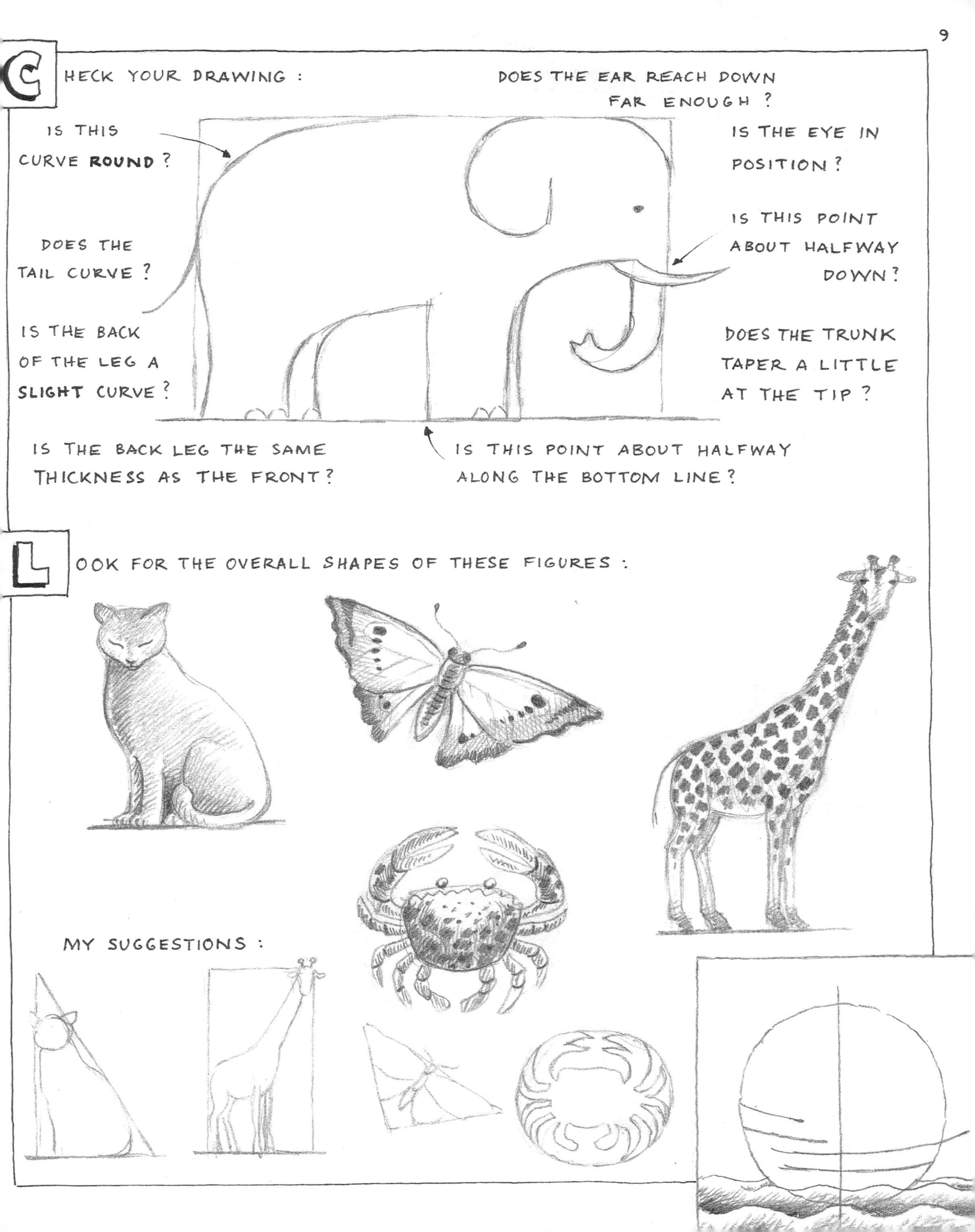
CHECK YOUR DRAWING :
DOES THE EAR REACH DOWN FAR ENOUGH ?
IS THIS CURVE ROUND ?
IS THE EYE IN POSITION ?
IS THIS POINT ABOUT HALFWAY DOWN ?
DOES THE TAIL CURVE ?
IS THE BACK OF THE LEG A SLIGHT CURVE ?
DOES THE TRUNK TAPER A LITTLE AT THE TIP ?
IS THE BACK LEG THE SAME THICKNESS AS THE FRONT ?
IS THIS POINT ABOUT HALFWAY ALONG THE BOTTOM LINE ?
LOOK FOR THE OVERALL SHAPES OF THESE FIGURES :
MY SUGGESTIONS :

NOTHER WAY TO SEE THE SIZE AND POSITION OF SHAPES IS TO USE A GRID.

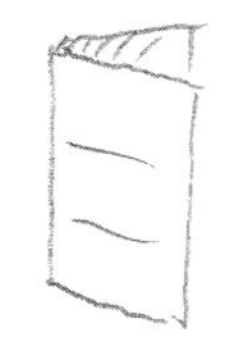

① HALVE YOUR SHEET LENGTHWAYS, ② AND AGAIN.

③ OPEN OUT AND HALVE WIDTHWAYS, ④ AND AGAIN.

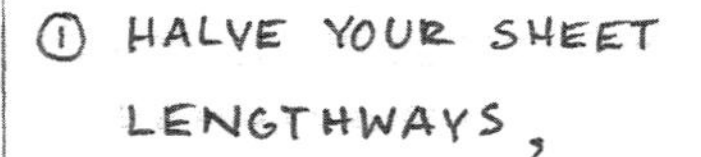

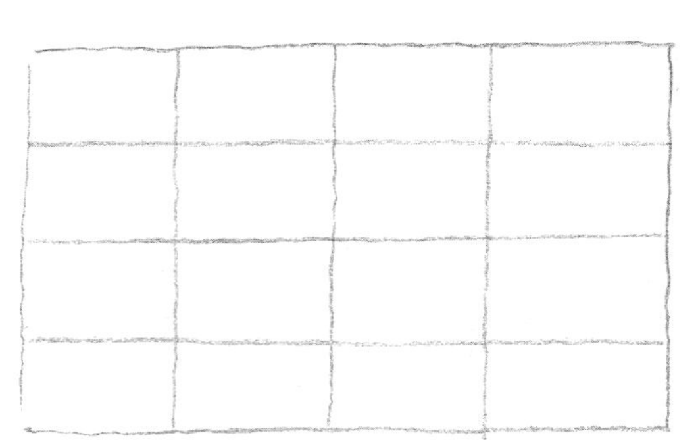

WHEN YOU OPEN YOUR SHEET, THE FOLD-LINES SHOULD MAKE A GRID LIKE THIS.

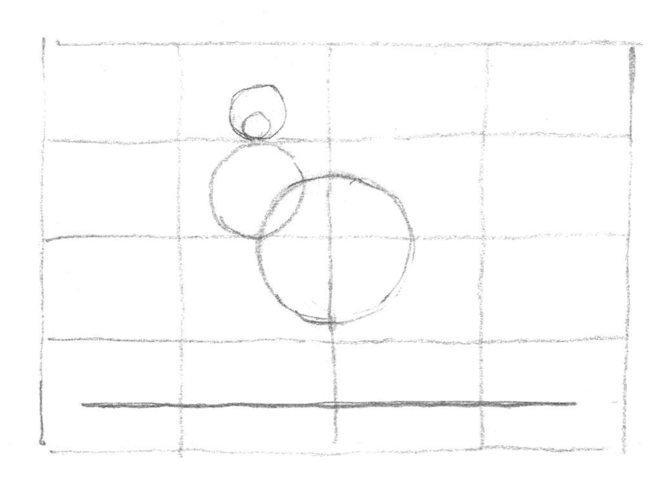

① LIGHTLY DRAW FOUR CIRCLES. NOTE THEIR **POSITION** AND **SIZE**. DRAW IN A GROUND LINE.

② DRAW 2 CURVES FOR THE TAIL, AND 2 FOR THE BODY. SEE WHERE THEY BEGIN AND END. DRAW A LINE FOR THE BACK LEG.

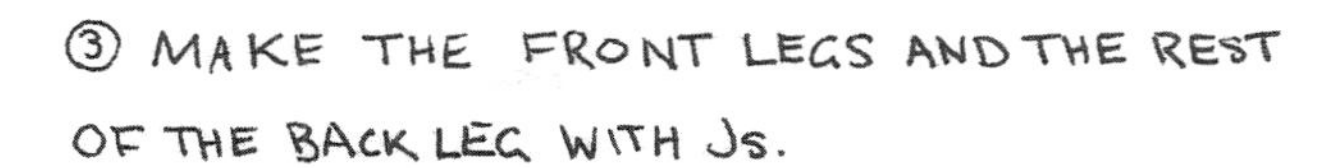

③ MAKE THE FRONT LEGS AND THE REST OF THE BACK LEG WITH Js.

MAKE EARS WITH LONG Ds, EYES WITH SMALL CIRCLES, AND NOSTRILS WITH 2 DASHES.

④ THICKEN THE FRONT LEGS AND ADD ANOTHER LEG BEHIND THE FIRST.
GO OVER THE LINES YOU WANT AND ERASE THE ONES YOU DON'T.

THE GREAT DUTCH ARTIST, VINCENT VAN GOGH, USED A GRID HE MADE WITH A WOODEN FRAME AND FOUR PIECES OF WIRE.

YOU CAN MAKE YOUR OWN GRID WITH A SHEET OF FLAT, CLEAR PLASTIC, SUCH AS THE LID OF A SHIRT-BOX OR TOY PACKAGING.
USE A RULER AND A PERMANENT MARKER TO DRAW THE LINES.
THE GRID ON THE PAPER YOU USE SHOULD HAVE THE SAME PROPORTIONS, EITHER FOLDED OR DRAWN.

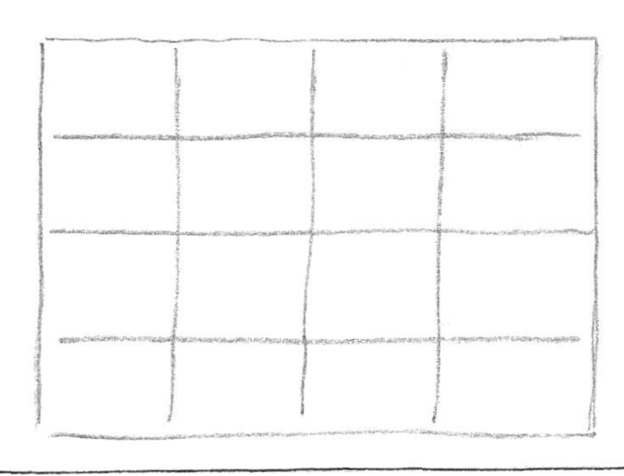

STICK THE PLASTIC ON A WINDOW TO DRAW THE SCENE OUTSIDE, OR LAY IT OVER A PICTURE IN A BOOK TO HELP YOU DRAW IT.

RY OUT THE OVERALL SHAPE APPROACH OR THE GRID APPROACH, OR BOTH, ON THESE FIGURES.

REMEMBER: PAPER AROUND THE RIGHT WAY, PENCIL SHARP, RELAX, LOOK, SEE, IMAGINE, DRAW LIGHTLY AND DON'T WORRY ABOUT MISTAKES.

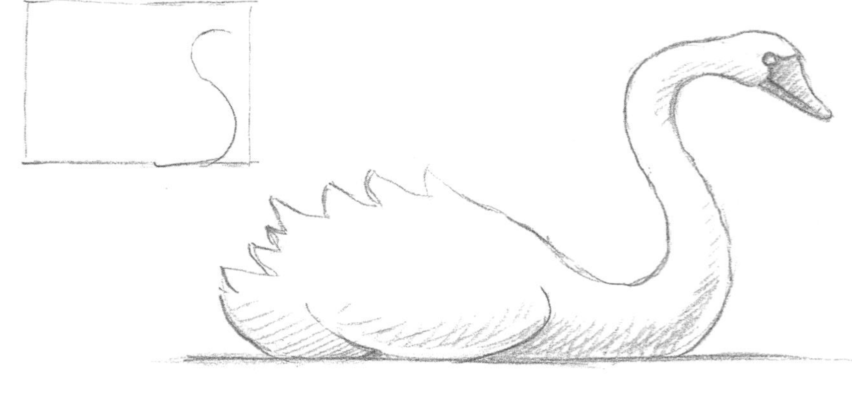

EOPLE THINK FACES ARE DIFFICULT TO DRAW, EVEN THOUGH WE PROBABLY SPEND MORE TIME LOOKING AT THEM THAN ANYTHING ELSE.

WE **LOOK**, BUT HOW WELL DO WE **SEE**?

I LOVE DRAWING FACES! THEY CAN **EXPRESS** SO MUCH – AND IT'S THE **LITTLE** LINES THAT DO IT. TRY THIS:

 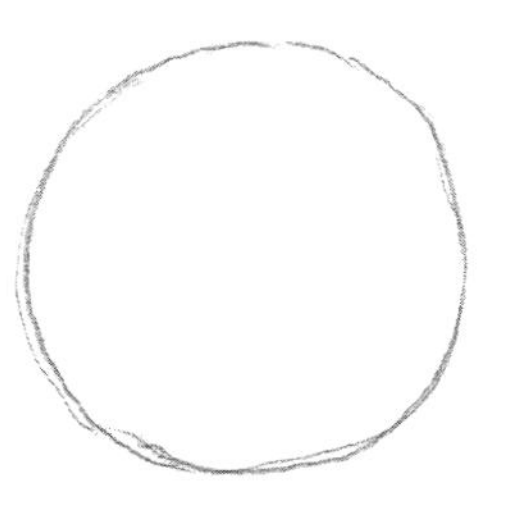  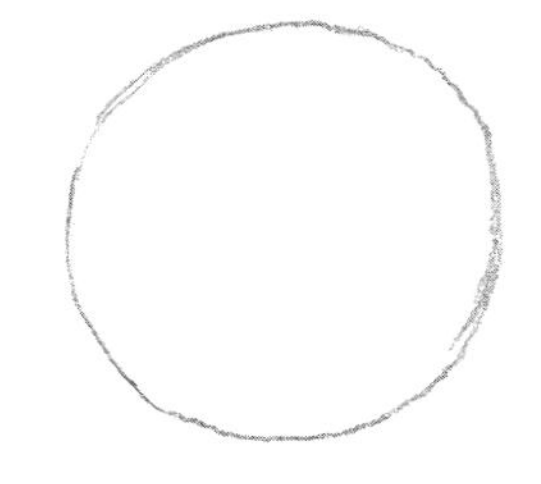

① DRAW 4 CIRCLES, ALL THE SAME SIZE.

② USE C's TO MAKE NOSES AND MOUTHS, ALL THE SAME.

③ NOW WITH AN a AND A DOT, SEE HOW THE EYES CHANGE WHOLE EXPRESSIONS!

RACTISE EXPRESSIONS IN FRONT OF THE MIRROR – LOOK FOR THE **LITTLE** LINES THAT CHANGE – ESPECIALLY AROUND THE EYES.

MOST FACES ARE OVAL LIKE AN EGG, ROUND AT THE TOP, NARROWER AT THE BOTTOM.

TRY DRAWING YOUR **OWN** FACE. YOU'LL NEED A MIRROR, OR A LARGE, FRONT-ON PHOTOGRAPH. BEGIN WITH AN OVAL.

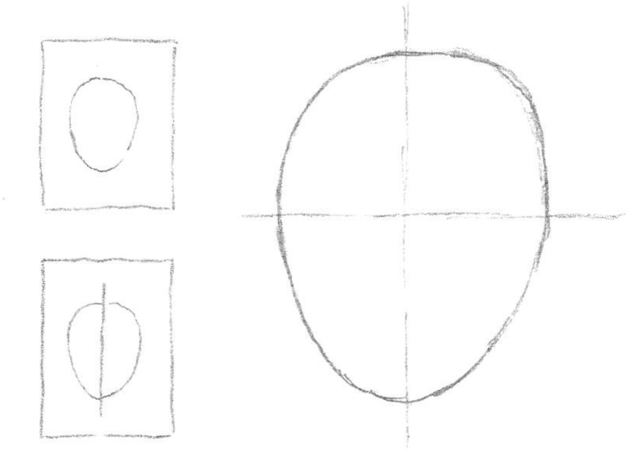

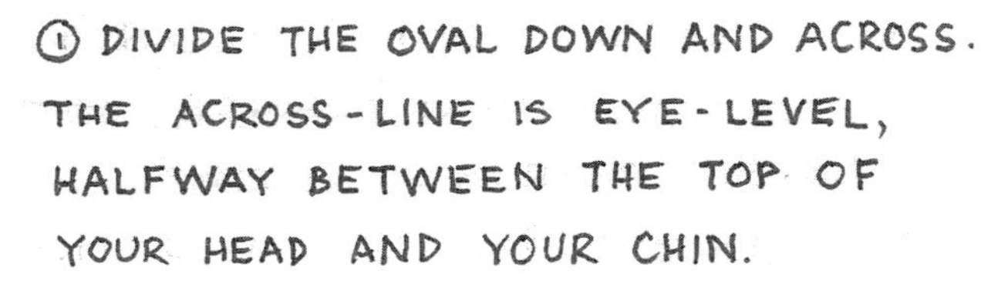

① DIVIDE THE OVAL DOWN AND ACROSS. THE ACROSS-LINE IS EYE-LEVEL, HALFWAY BETWEEN THE TOP OF YOUR HEAD AND YOUR CHIN.

② IS YOUR CHIN POINTY, SQUARE, OR ROUND? DRAW IT IN. NOW LOOK FOR THE TWO LINES OF YOUR NECK, AND DRAW THEM.

REMEMBER, YOU'RE LOOKING FOR SIMPLE, **OVERALL SHAPES**. DRAW LIGHTLY AND DON'T WORRY ABOUT DETAILS. DETAILS COME LATER.

③ LOOK FOR THE OVERALL SHAPE OF YOUR HAIR. USE THE CENTRE-LINES TO GUIDE YOU. DON'T TRY TO DRAW EVERY HAIR, JUST THE SHAPE.

MAKE TWO DOTS HALFWAY BETWEEN THE CENTRE LINE AND THE EDGES OF THE OVAL. THESE WILL BE YOUR EYEBALLS.

YES! OF ALL THE THINGS YOU'LL EVER DRAW, NOTHING WILL BE AS MUCH OF A MYSTERY AS EYES.
THERE ARE **BILLIONS** OF EYES, AND NO TWO ARE THE SAME.
WHAT SHAPE ARE **YOUR** EYES?

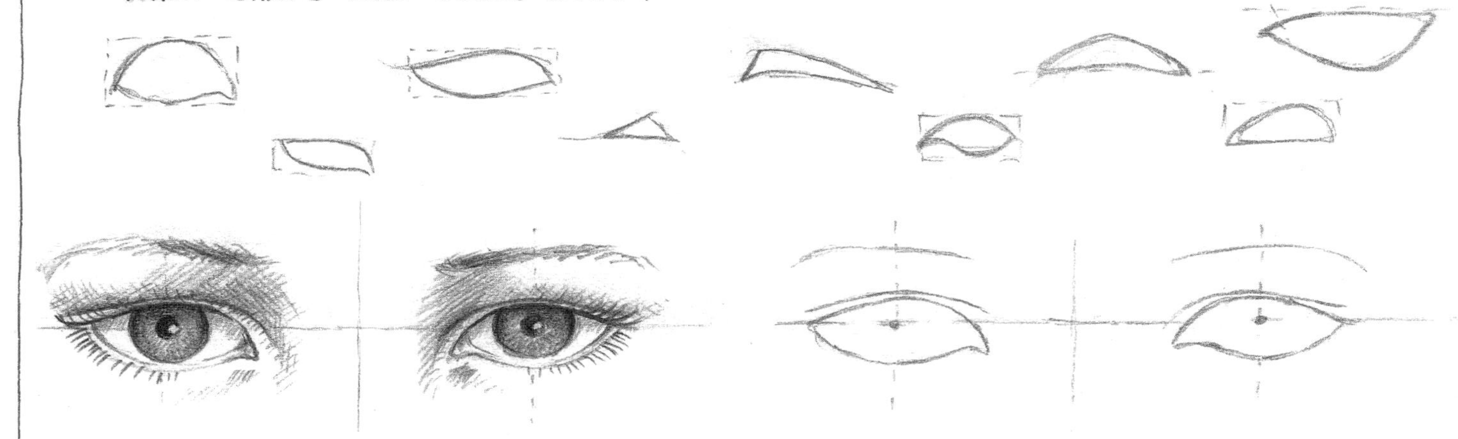

LOOK FOR THE SHAPES. DON'T TRY TO DRAW SHADOWS YET. FIND THE EYELASH LINES THAT MAKE THE OVERALL SHAPE.

USE THE EYEBALL DOT AS A GUIDE TO POSITION THE SHAPE OF YOUR EYES. YOUR EYES ARE ABOUT ONE EYEWIDTH APART.

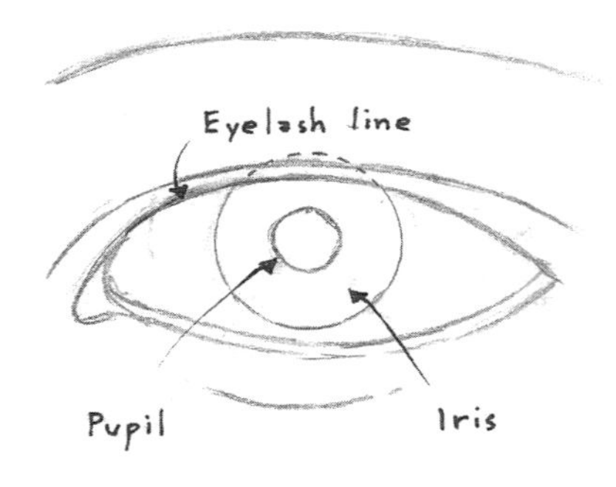

DON'T TRY TO DRAW EVERY EYELASH OR EYEBROW HAIR – JUST GET THE **LINE** RIGHT.
NOTICE WHERE THE CIRCLE OF YOUR **IRIS** SITS – DOES IT TOUCH THE EYELASH LINE?
DRAW IN THE PUPIL – BLACK, WITH A DOT OF WHITE REFLECTION.

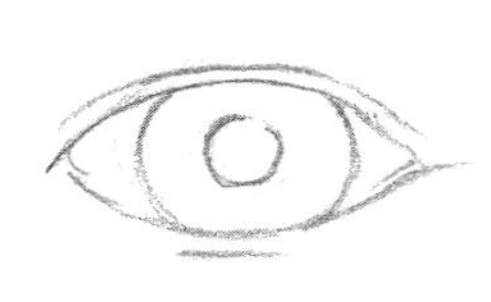

THE TIP OF YOUR **NOSE** IS A LITTLE LESS THAN HALFWAY FROM THE EYELINE TO THE CHIN
YOUR **MOUTH** IS ABOUT A THIRD OF THE WAY FROM THE NOSE TO THE CHIN.
MARK THESE LIGHTLY ON THE CENTRE LINE.

YOUR NOSE IS ABOUT AS WIDE, AT THE TIP, AS THE DISTANCE BETWEEN YOUR EYES.

YOUR MOUTH IS ABOUT AS WIDE AS THE DISTANCE BETWEEN THE **CENTRES** OF YOUR EYES.

LOOK FOR THE LINES AROUND YOUR NOSTRILS. IGNORE THE SHADOWS; DRAW THE SIMPLE CURVES.

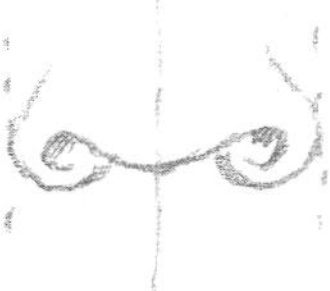

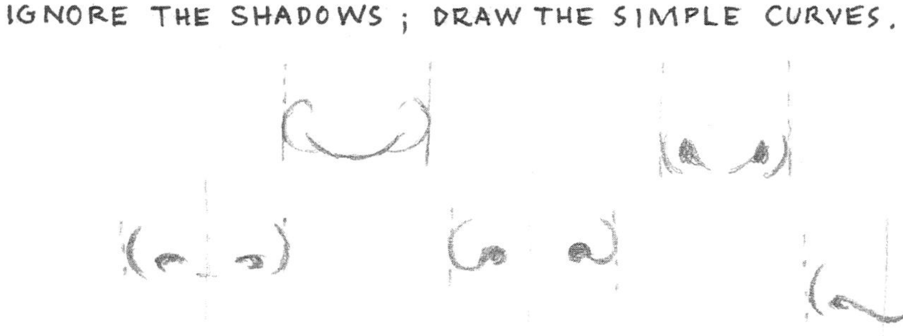

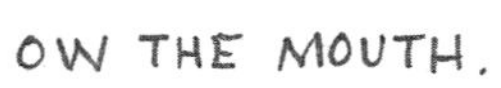

NOW THE MOUTH.

LOOK AT THE LINE WHERE THE LIPS MEET. IS IT STRAIGHT? DOES IT CURVE DOWN? UP? DOWN **AND** UP? DRAW IT IN LIGHTLY.

LOOK AT THE OVERALL SHAPE OF YOUR LIPS. IS THE TOP LIP AS THICK AS THE BOTTOM LIP? LOOK FOR THE **SIMPLE** CURVES AND DRAW THEM **LIGHTLY**.

THE MIDDLE LINE WHERE THE LIPS MEET IS GENERALLY THE DARKEST. THE OUTLINE IS NOT SO MUCH A LINE AS A CHANGE OF COLOUR. KEEP IT **SOFT**.

DRAW IN ANY OTHER DEFINITE LINES, LIKE DIMPLES, MOLES, OR GLASSES.

IF YOU CAN SEE THE EARS, DRAW THEM IN. THEIR TOPS ARE LEVEL WITH THE TOPS OF YOUR EYES, AND THEY END LEVEL WITH THE SPACE BETWEEN YOUR NOSE AND YOUR MOUTH.

NOW TRY A PROFILE. BEGIN WITH A **CIRCLE**. (HEADS ARE WIDER SIDE-ON THAN FACE-ON.)

② DIVIDE IT LIGHTLY DOWN AND ACROSS.

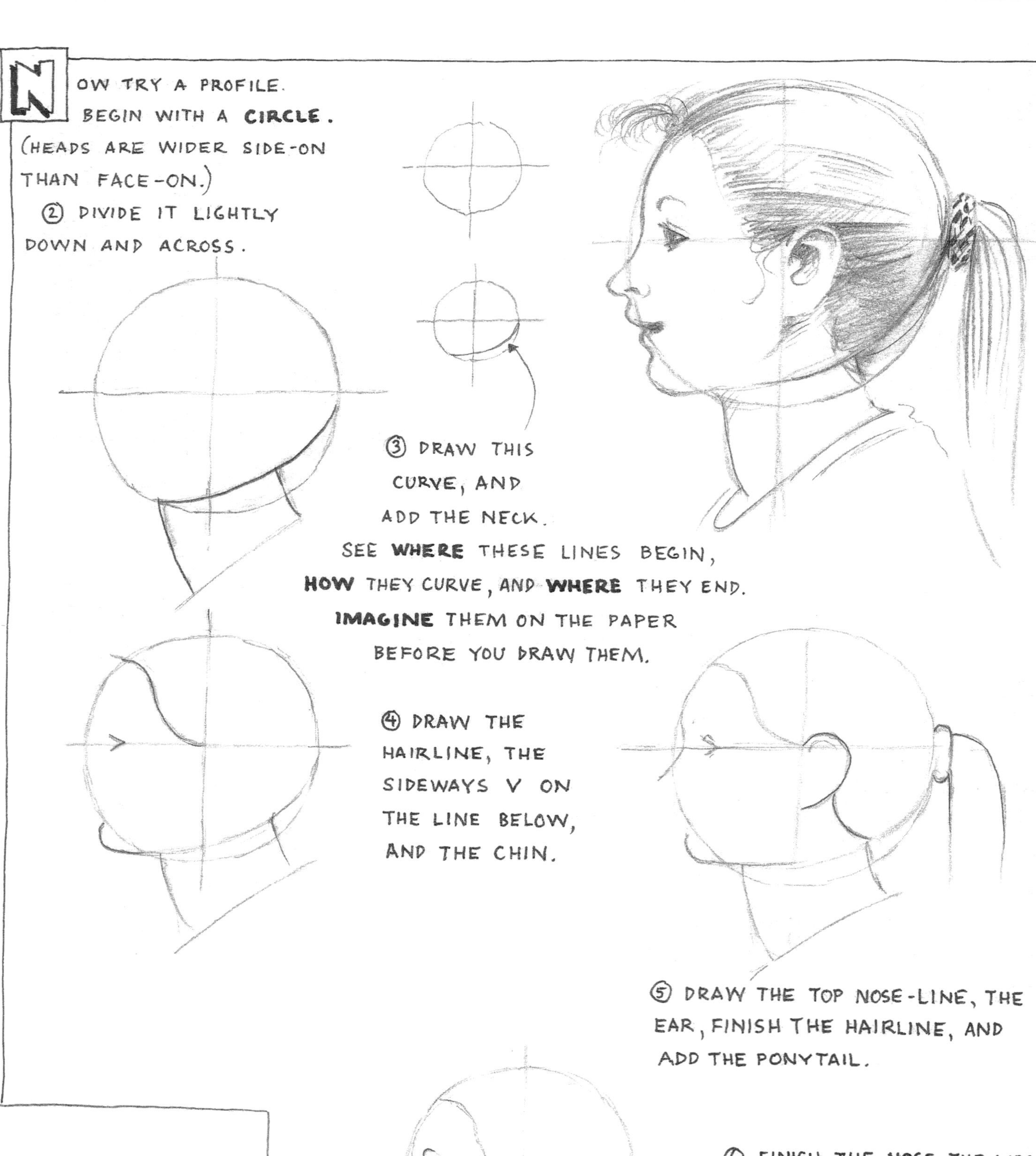

③ DRAW THIS CURVE, AND ADD THE NECK.

SEE **WHERE** THESE LINES BEGIN, **HOW** THEY CURVE, AND **WHERE** THEY END. **IMAGINE** THEM ON THE PAPER BEFORE YOU DRAW THEM.

④ DRAW THE HAIRLINE, THE SIDEWAYS V ON THE LINE BELOW, AND THE CHIN.

⑤ DRAW THE TOP NOSE-LINE, THE EAR, FINISH THE HAIRLINE, AND ADD THE PONYTAIL.

⑥ FINISH THE NOSE, THE LIPS AND THE EYES BY LOOKING CAREFULLY AT THE PICTURE ABOVE.

HEADS ARE ATTACHED TO BODIES OF ALL SHAPES AND SIZES, BUT THE SAME BASIC PROPORTIONS APPLY TO US ALL.

FOR EXAMPLE:

THERE ARE ABOUT SEVEN HEAD-LENGTHS TO A BODY.

OUR LEGS MAKE UP ALMOST HALF OUR BODY LENGTH.

WRIST TO SHOULDER IS AS LONG AS KNEE TO HIP.

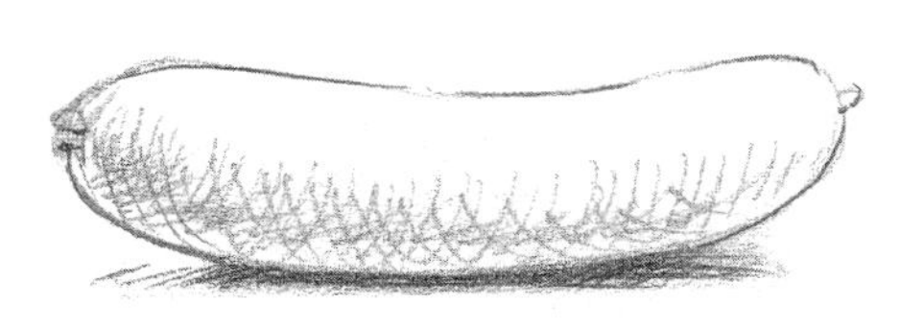

I LEARNED TO DRAW BODIES BY MAKING SAUSAGES!

SAUSAGES HELP YOU TO SEE ALL THE DIFFERENT SHAPES AND SIZES THAT MAKE UP OUR BODIES, AND HOW ALL THE BITS ARE JOINED TOGETHER.

THE TORSO IS MADE UP OF THREE SAUSAGES: THE CHEST, THE STOMACH, AND THE PELVIS.

THESE ARE CONNECTED, FROM THE HEAD TO THE PELVIS, BY THE SPINE, LIKE A CENTRELINE.

ALL THE OTHER SAUSAGES ARE CONNECTED TO EACH OTHER AND TO THE TORSO, BY BALL JOINTS.

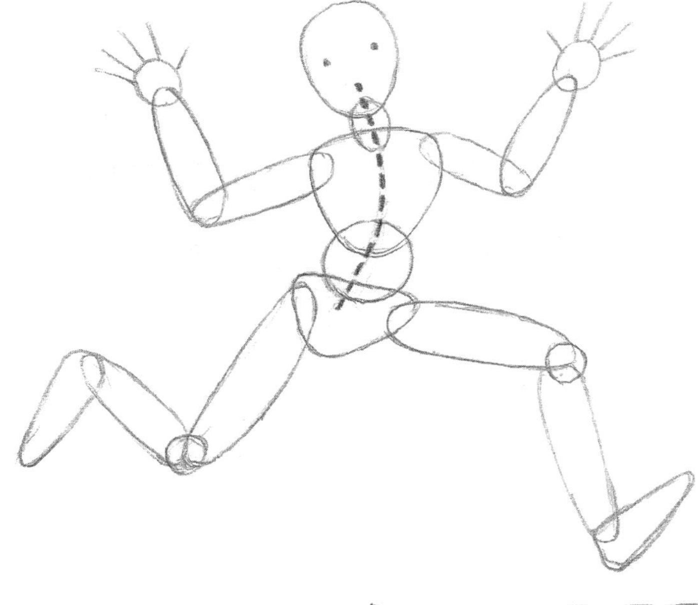

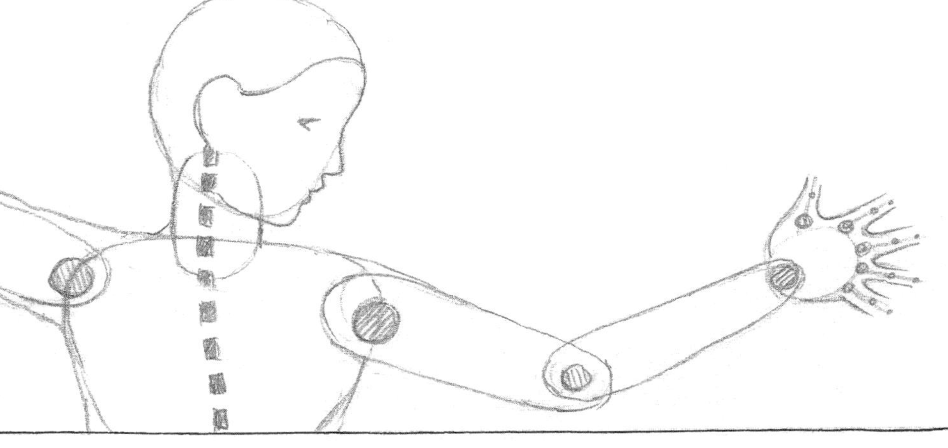

YOU'VE SEEN ALREADY THAT THE SHAPE OF OUR HEAD CHANGES FROM AN OVAL WHEN SEEN FROM THE FRONT, TO A CIRCLE WHEN SEEN FROM THE SIDE.

OTHER PARTS OF OUR BODIES CHANGE TOO, FROM THE FRONT TO THE SIDE - MAINLY THE CHEST, PELVIS, HANDS AND FEET

LOOK FOR THE CHANGES IN THESE SAUSAGE FIGURES.

THE WAY I DRAW HANDS AND FEET IS THE SAME AS THE WAY I DRAW EVERYTHING ELSE: BY LOOKING FOR THE OVERALL SHAPE.

HANDS CAN BE CIRCULAR,

OR TRIANGULAR,

OR RECTANGULAR,

OR A COMBINATION.

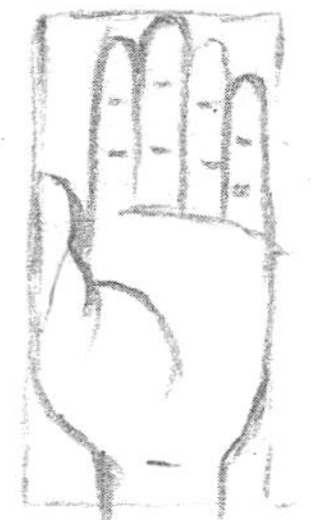

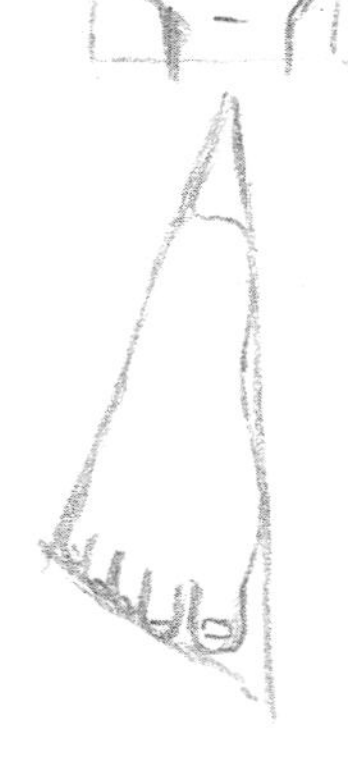

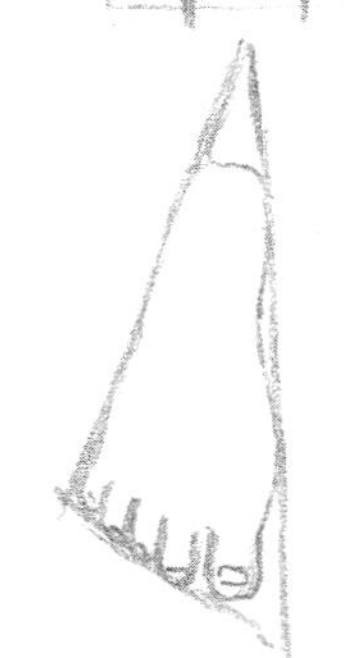

FEET ARE OFTEN TRIANGULAR,

OR A COMBINATION, WITH CURVES.

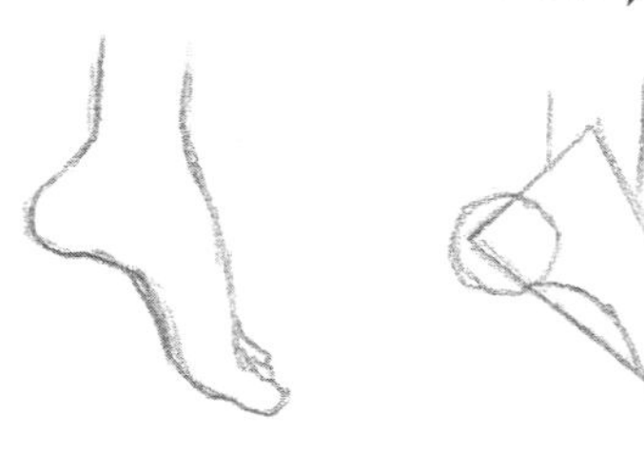

TRY DRAWING THESE SAUSAGE FIGURES. DRAW LIGHTLY SO THAT WHEN YOU HAVE THE POSITION RIGHT YOU CAN GO OVER IT WITH DETAILS.

BEGIN WITH THE SIMPLEST OVERALL SHAPE, OR LINES, AND BUILD THE FIGURE STEP BY STEP.

THESE SIMPLE-TO-MAKE FIGURES ARE A USEFUL (AND FUN) GUIDE TO DRAWING DIFFERENT POSITIONS.

TRACE OR DRAW THE SHAPES ONTO LIGHT CARDBOARD AND CUT THEM OUT.

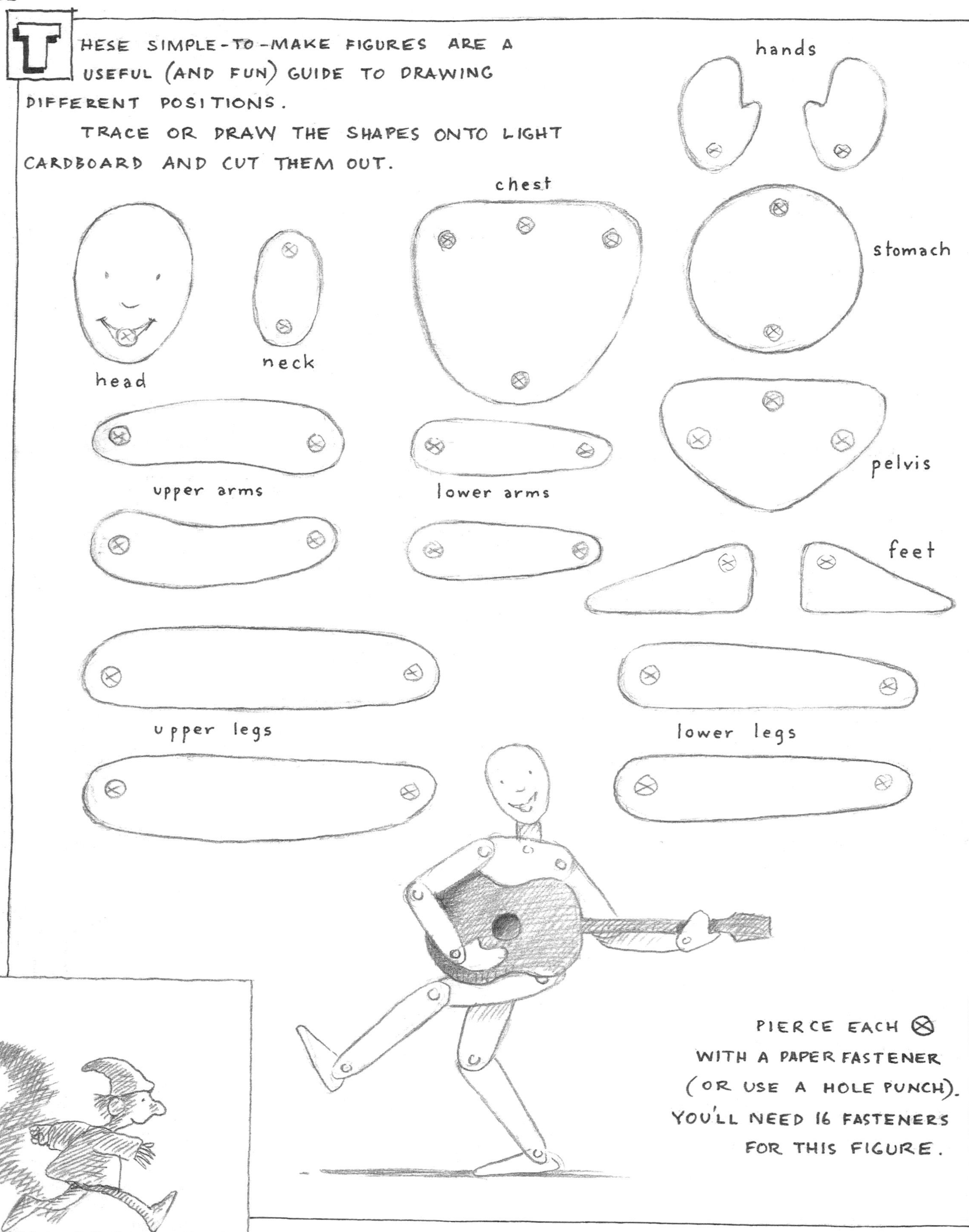

PIERCE EACH ⊗ WITH A PAPER FASTENER (OR USE A HOLE PUNCH). YOU'LL NEED 16 FASTENERS FOR THIS FIGURE.

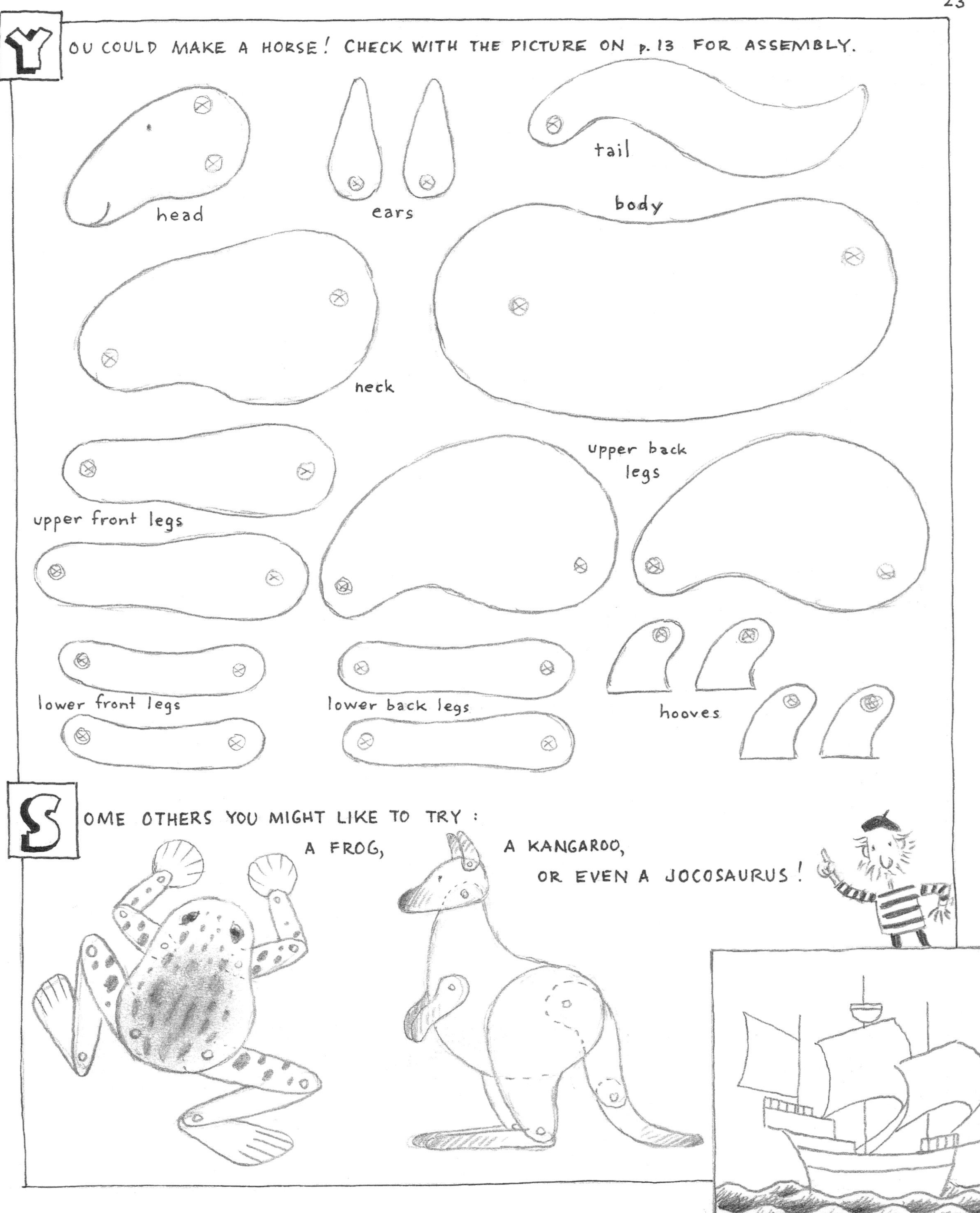
Y
OU COULD MAKE A HORSE! CHECK WITH THE PICTURE ON p. 13 FOR ASSEMBLY.
head
ears
tail
body
neck
upper front legs
upper back legs
lower front legs
lower back legs
hooves
S
OME OTHERS YOU MIGHT LIKE TO TRY :
A FROG,
A KANGAROO,
OR EVEN A JOCOSAURUS!

HINGS APPEAR TO GROW SMALLER, AND CLOSER TOGETHER, THE FURTHER AWAY THEY ARE FROM YOU.

THIS IS CALLED PERSPECTIVE.

WRITE THE WORD PERSPECTIVE, WITH DOUBLE SPACE BETWEEN THE LETTERS, AND DRAW A LINE BELOW IT. PLACE A DOT ON THE LINE BELOW THE E.

P E R S P E C T I V E

JOIN THE LETTERS TO THE DOT, BEGINNING WITH THE E ABOVE IT AND MOVING OUTWARDS EACH WAY. USE A RULER IF YOU LIKE.

WHAT YOU'VE DONE IS YOU'VE GIVEN **DEPTH** TO THE WORD.

THIS FEELING OF DEPTH IS WHAT PERSPECTIVE IS ALL ABOUT.

YOU CAN DO IT WITH STRAIGHT LINES, OR OVERLAPPING SHAPES, OR DIFFERENT TONES, OR A COMBINATION OF ALL OF THESE.

HICHEVER WAY YOU DO IT, PERSPECTIVE IS ABOUT THINGS BECOMING SMALLER AND CLOSER TOGETHER TOWARDS A DISTANT POINT OR POINTS ALONG A LINE.

THIS LINE IS CALLED THE HORIZON LINE.

IF YOU STAND ON THE DECK OF A BOAT AT SEA, THE HORIZON LINE IS WHERE THE OCEAN MEETS THE SKY.

IF THERE ARE PEOPLE AROUND YOU **AT YOUR OWN LEVEL** (STANDING OR SITTING), THE HORIZON LINE IS THE AVERAGE EYE-LEVEL OF THESE PEOPLE.

THE HORIZON LINE IS THE CURVATURE OF THE EARTH, AND IS THE BEST GUIDE WE HAVE FOR PERSPECTIVE.

IF THERE ARE NO PEOPLE AROUND, OR YOU'RE NOT ON A BOAT AT SEA, JUST POINT STRAIGHT AHEAD, WITH YOUR FINGER AT EYE-LEVEL.

YOU'RE POINTING AT THE HORIZON LINE.

DRAW A SQUARE WITH A LINE BEHIND IT. (THIS WILL BE YOUR HORIZON LINE.)

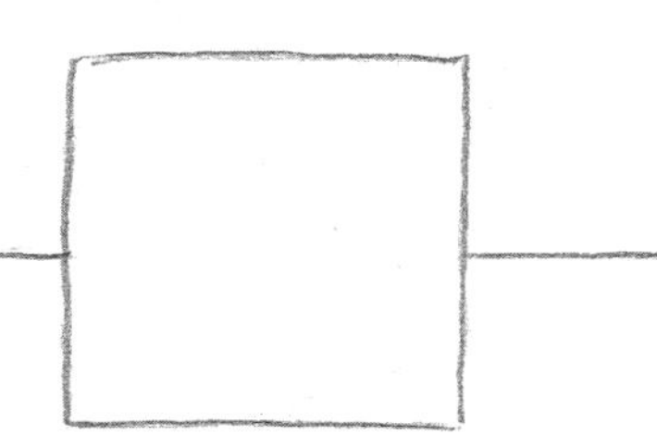

MAKE A DOT ON THE LINE AND CONNECT THE DOT TO THE SQUARE

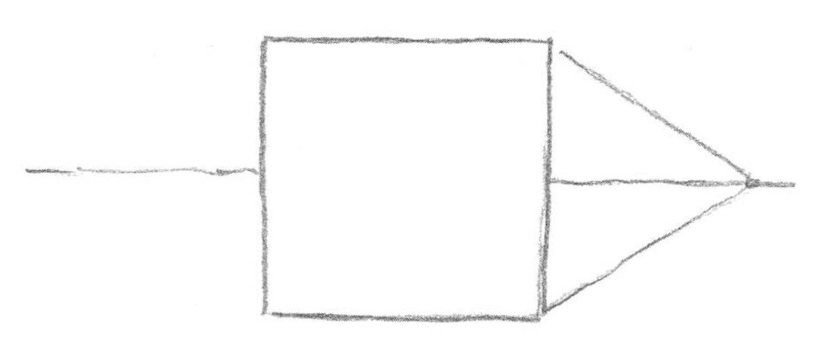

NOW MAKE A VERTICAL LINE BETWEEN THE LAST TWO LINES.

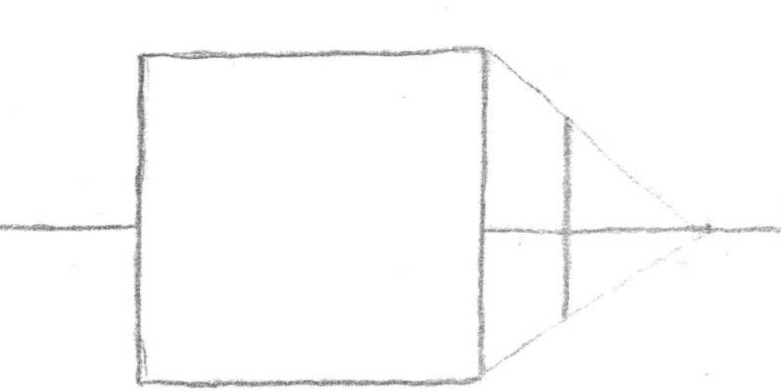

YOU'VE GIVEN DEPTH TO THE SQUARE – IT'S BECOME A BOX!

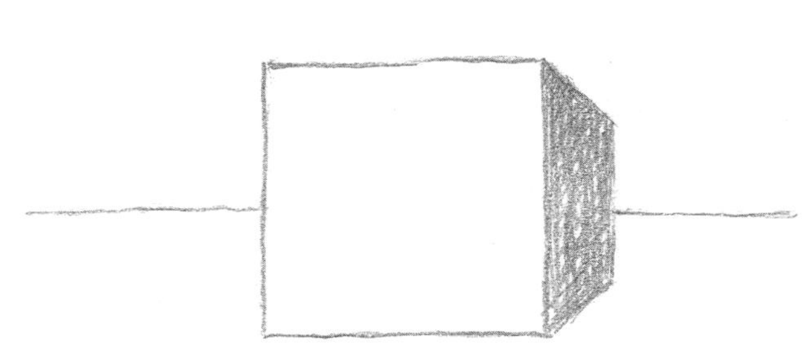

NOTICE THAT THE LAST VERTICAL LINE YOU DREW IS SHORTER THAN THE TWO AT THE FRONT. IT'S SHORTER BECAUSE IT'S "FURTHER AWAY".

NOW, YOU **KNOW** THAT THE SIDE OF THE BOX IS **SQUARE**, BUT THE SHAPE THAT YOU **SEE** IS A **TRAPEZOID** (**TRAP**-EZOID).

IT'S LIKE WHEN A DOOR OPENS, AND YOU **KNOW** THAT THE DOOR IS A RECTANGLE, BUT WHAT YOU **SEE** IS A DOOR SHAPED LIKE A TRAPEZOID.

IF YOU WERE TO CONTINUE THE LINES AT THE TOP AND BOTTOM OF THE DOOR, THEY WOULD MEET (YOU GUESSED IT!) ON THE HORIZON LINE.

OPEN THE DOOR AND **SEE**!

LOOK AND SEE THE DIFFERENT SHAPES THINGS BECOME WHEN THEY'RE GIVEN DEPTH. SQUARES AND RECTANGLES BECOME TRAPEZOIDS. CIRCLES BECOME OVALS.

THE NEW SHAPES ARE NO MORE DIFFICULT TO DRAW – THEY'RE STILL MADE OF BITS OF LETTERS AND NUMBERS – YOU ONLY NEED TO **SEE** THEM. TRY THESE:

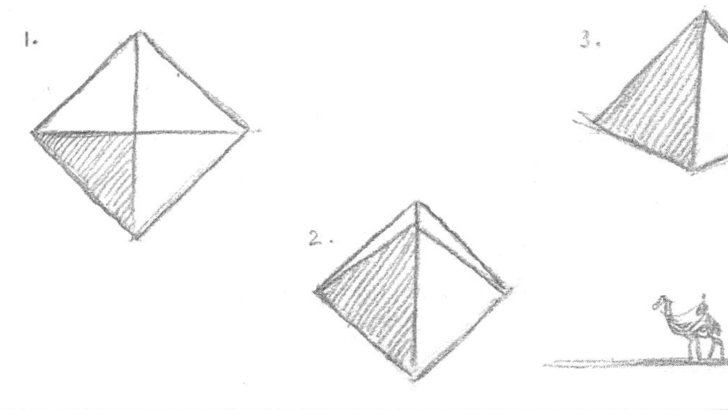

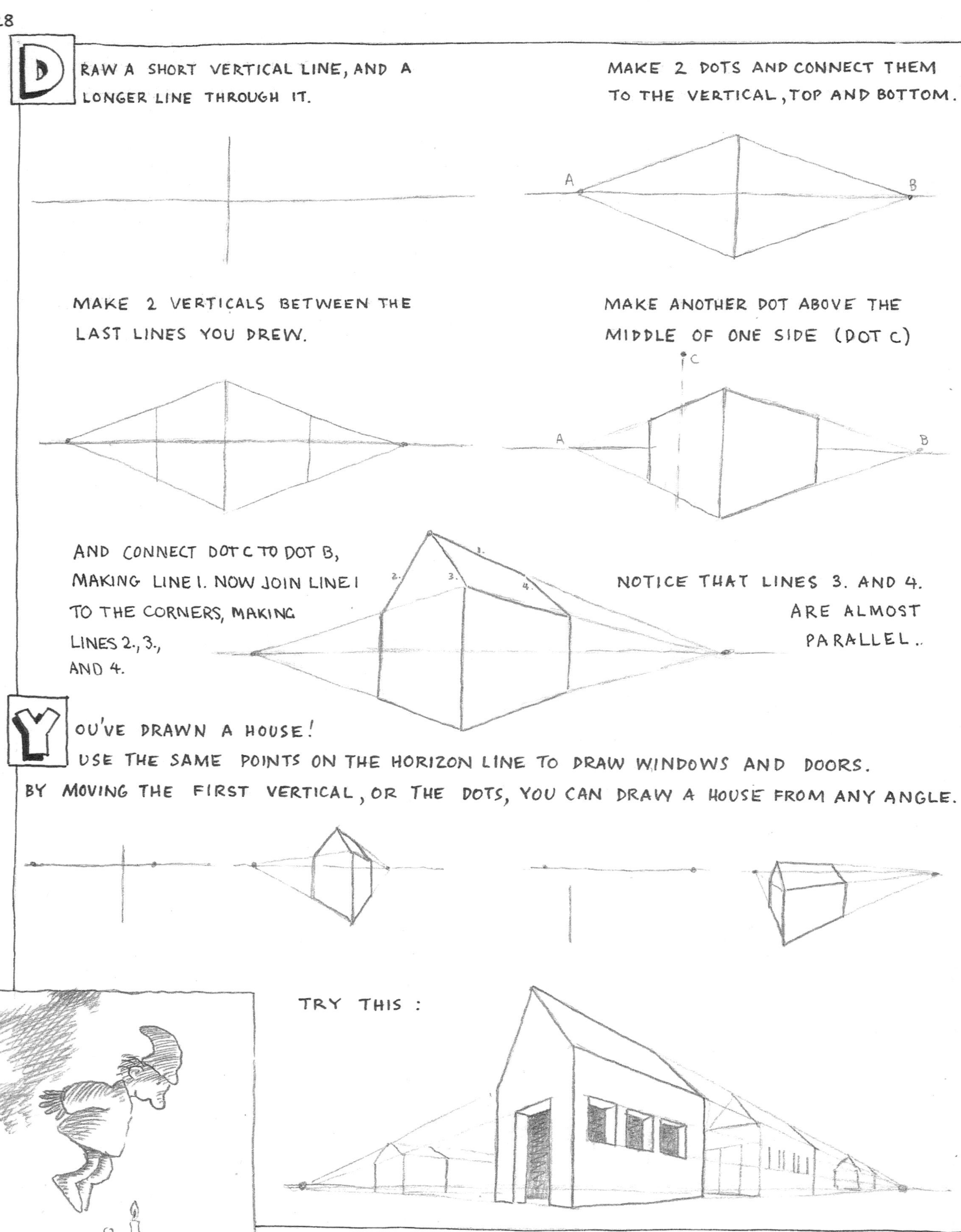
DRAW A SHORT VERTICAL LINE, AND A LONGER LINE THROUGH IT.
MAKE 2 DOTS AND CONNECT THEM TO THE VERTICAL, TOP AND BOTTOM.
A
B
MAKE 2 VERTICALS BETWEEN THE LAST LINES YOU DREW.
MAKE ANOTHER DOT ABOVE THE MIDDLE OF ONE SIDE (DOT C)
C
A
B
AND CONNECT DOT C TO DOT B, MAKING LINE 1. NOW JOIN LINE 1 TO THE CORNERS, MAKING LINES 2., 3., AND 4.
1.
2.
3.
4.
NOTICE THAT LINES 3. AND 4. ARE ALMOST PARALLEL..
YOU'VE DRAWN A HOUSE!
USE THE SAME POINTS ON THE HORIZON LINE TO DRAW WINDOWS AND DOORS.
BY MOVING THE FIRST VERTICAL, OR THE DOTS, YOU CAN DRAW A HOUSE FROM ANY ANGLE.
TRY THIS :

AKE A MUG AND LOOK AT IT SIDE-ON.
IT'S A RECTANGLE WITH AN EAR!
DRAW YOUR MUG LIKE SO:

NOW TILT THE MUG SLIGHTLY TOWARDS YOU.

THE BOTTOM EDGE HAS BECOME A CURVE, AND THE TOP HAS BECOME AN OVAL.
LOOK FOR CHANGES IN THE SHAPE OF THE HANDLE TOO.

TILT THE MUG AGAIN, UNTIL YOU CAN JUST SEE THE CURVE OF THE BOTTOM INSIDE.
DRAW THIS VIEW, BEGINNING WITH OVERLAPPING OVALS.
NOTICE THAT THE BOTTOM OVAL IS SLIGHTLY SMALLER. CONNECT THE SIDES AND ADD THE HANDLE.

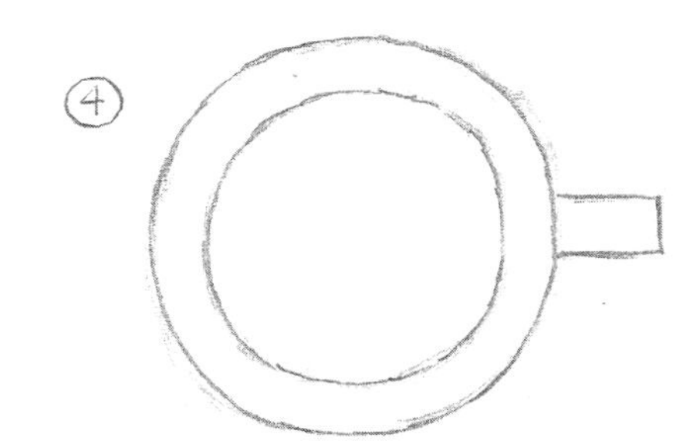

FINALLY, DRAW THE MUG FROM DIRECTLY ABOVE. TWO CIRCLES, ONE WITHIN THE OTHER, AND A RECTANGLE.

PERSPECTIVE IS NO MORE DIFFICULT THAN ANY OTHER AREA OF DRAWING. YOU NEED TO **LOOK**, CAREFULLY, AND DRAW THE SIMPLE SHAPES FIRST. YOU'LL GET BETTER AND BETTER, BUT YOU HAVE TO PRACTISE, PRACTISE, PRACTISE!

WE'VE SEEN WHAT CAN BE DONE WITH LINES AND SHAPES, NOW LET'S FINISH THE PICTURE, WITH LIGHT AND SHADE.

LINES CAN MAKE THE SHAPE, BUT LIGHT AND SHADE GIVE THE SHAPE **FORM**.

THE LIGHT ON THE MUG COMES FROM ABOVE RIGHT, AND CASTS SHADOWS TO THE LEFT.

NOTICE THE SHADOW **INSIDE** THE MUG, AND ON THE HANDLE.

ON A CURVED SURFACE LIKE A MUG OR A BALL, THE SHADING IS GRADUAL AND EVEN, FROM THE DARKEST TONE TO THE LIGHTEST.

ON SOMETHING MADE OF FLAT SURFACES, THE SHADING IS STILL GRADUAL, FROM DARK TO LIGHT, BUT IT CHANGES FROM SURFACE TO SURFACE, SHAPE TO SHAPE, EACH SHAPE HAVING ITS OWN EVEN TONE.

MANY THINGS YOU DRAW HAVE A COMBINATION OF CURVED SURFACES AND FLAT SURFACES.

FACES, FOR EXAMPLE.

SO YOU NEED TO BE ABLE TO SHADE GRADUALLY AND EVENLY, FROM DARK TO LIGHT.

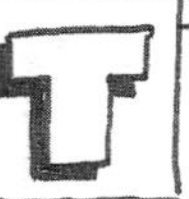HERE ARE MANY WAYS TO SHADE WITH A PENCIL:

CONTINUOUS TONE. HOLD THE PENCIL ALMOST FLAT TO THE PAPER AND MOVE IT AROUND WITH GENTLE CONTINUOUS MOTIONS, PRESSING HARDER FOR THE DARKEST TONES.

DOTS. (TIME CONSUMING AND POSSIBLY BORING.) THE TONE IS DARKEST WHERE THE DOTS ARE CLOSEST TOGETHER.

COMBINATION SOLID AND LINE. THIS IS OK FOR SOME THINGS, BUT TENDS TO LOOK A BIT MECHANICAL.

CARTOON. THIS MIGHT LOOK SIMPLE BUT ISN'T. IT'S REALLY ONLY SUITABLE FOR CERTAIN KINDS OF DRAWING.

SMUDGING. THIS CAN PRODUCE SOME BEAUTIFUL RESULTS, BUT IS DIFFICULT TO CONTROL AND CAN BE MESSY.

PARALLEL LINES AND DASHES. THIS IS SIMILAR TO THE TECHNIQUE OF ENGRAVING USED A LOT IN PRINTING LAST CENTURY. YOU NEED PATIENCE AND A VERY STEADY HAND.

CROSS-HATCHING. THIS IS MY FAVOURITE. IT'S LOOSE, EASY TO CONTROL, AND CREATES AN INTERESTING SURFACE.
BUT, LIKE ANYTHING ELSE, IT NEEDS **PRACTICE**!

CROSS-HATCHING, LIKE LINES, SHAPES AND PERSPECTIVE, LIKE **SEEING**, NEEDS PRACTICE, BUT YOU **CAN** DO IT, AND ONCE YOU'VE GOT THE HANG OF IT, YOU CAN DRAW **ANYTHING**!

THE MAIN THING IS TO RELAX, AND DRAW QUICK, EVEN STROKES.

BEGIN BY MAKING FIVE CIRCLES.

SHADE ALL THE CIRCLES IN THE DIRECTION SHOWN.

IMAGINE A LINE FROM 7 O'CLOCK TO 1 O'CLOCK, AND MAKE YOUR STROKES PARALLEL TO IT.

LEFT-HANDERS MIGHT FEEL MORE COMFORTABLE GOING FROM FIVE O'CLOCK TO ELEVEN O'CLOCK, AND CONTINUING IN AN ANTI-CLOCKWISE DIRECTION.

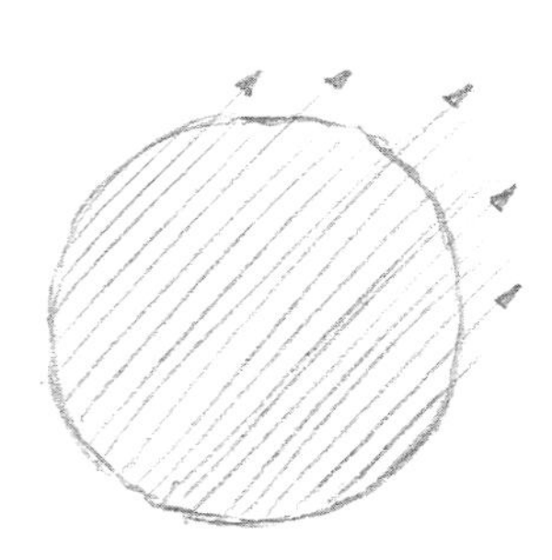

NOW MAKE STROKES ON THE NEXT FOUR CIRCLES IN THIS DIRECTION (EIGHT O'CLOCK TO TWO).

BE LOOSE, DON'T WORRY ABOUT THE CIRCLE - IT'S ONLY THERE AS A GUIDE.

KEEP GOING AROUND THE "CLOCK" UNTIL ALL THE CIRCLES ARE HATCHED, AND YOU'LL HAVE A SEQUENCE LIKE THIS:

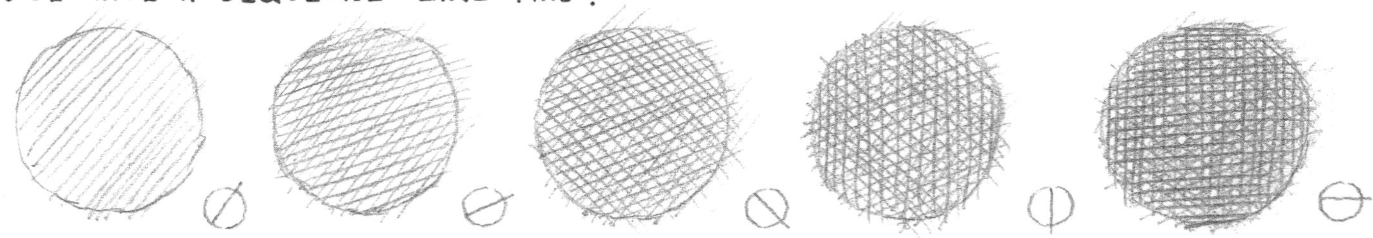

WHAT YOU HAVE DONE IS CROSS-HATCHED FIVE MAJOR TONES IN THE GRADATION FROM LIGHT TO DARK.

YOU DON'T HAVE TO STICK TO THE **EXACT** ANGLES I'VE SHOWN HERE.

THE MAIN THING IS THAT EACH NEW SET OF LINES MAKES THE TONE DARKER.

NOW MAKE A VERY LONG RECTANGLE.
LEAVE A WHITE SPACE AT THE LEFT, AND HATCH ALL THE WAY TO THE OTHER END.

MOVE A SPACE TO THE RIGHT AND HATCH ACROSS THE FIRST LINES.

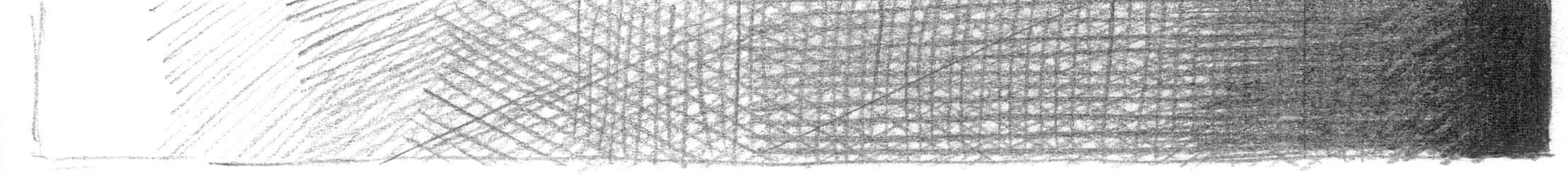

KEEP MOVING A SPACE TO THE RIGHT AT A TIME UNTIL YOU'VE HATCHED IN ALL DIRECTIONS, AND FILL THE REMAINING SECTION WITH SOLID PENCIL (BLACK).

THIS IS A **CONTINUOUS** CHANGE OF TONE, AND CAN BE USED TO SHADE CURVES – FACES, BALLS, CUPS, WHEELS, CARS, AEROPLANES – EVEN THE SKY!

TRY IT OUT ON YOUR ELEPHANT!
DECIDE WHERE THE LIGHT IS COMING FROM, AND **IMAGINE** IT – ON THE ROUND BACK, THE BUMPY HEAD, THE FLAT EAR.

IMAGINE WHERE IT WOULD BE DARKEST, AND WHERE THE LIGHT WOULD FALL.

IMAGINE ALSO WHERE THE SHADOWS WOULD BE.

NOTHER KIND OF CROSS-HATCHING, WHICH SHOWS THE ROUNDNESS OF THINGS EVEN MORE, USES **CURVED** STROKES.

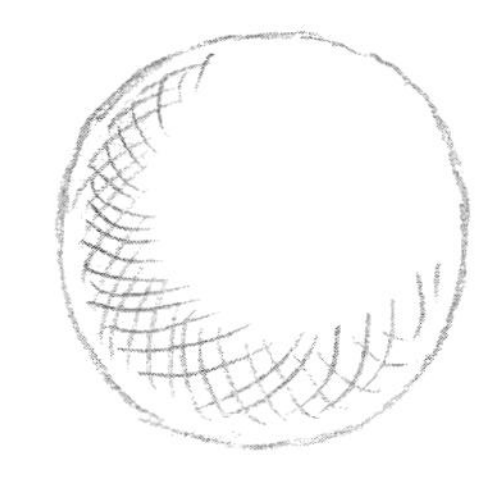
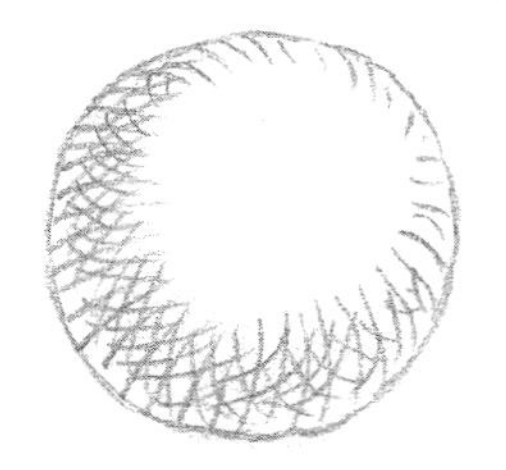

NOW LET'S HAVE ANOTHER LOOK IN THE MIRROR, OR AT YOUR PHOTO, AND THE DRAWING YOU MADE OF YOUR OWN FACE.

THE LINES ARE ALL THERE, SO ALL YOU NEED NOW ARE THE TONES.

A GOOD WAY TO **SEE** TONES IS TO **SQUINT**.

SQUINTING CUTS OUT ALL THE DETAIL – YOU SEE THE SIMPLE SHAPES OF LIGHT AND DARK. WHAT SHAPES DO YOU SEE?

HERE THE LIGHT IS COMING FROM ABOVE-RIGHT. THE LIGHTEST PARTS ARE LEFT WHITE, AND THE DARKEST PARTS ARE CROSS-HATCHED THREE OR FOUR TIMES.

NOW HATCH THE MIDDLE TONES. KEEP SQUINTING; LOOK FOR THE SIMPLE SHAPE OF EACH TONE, OR THE GRADUAL CHANGE FROM LIGHT TO DARK OVER THE CURVES.

IF YOU FEEL THAT CROSS-HATCHING ISN'T "SMOOTH" ENOUGH (FOR THINGS LIKE PLANES OR CARS), TRY THIS:

BEGIN WITH YOUR LINE DRAWING.

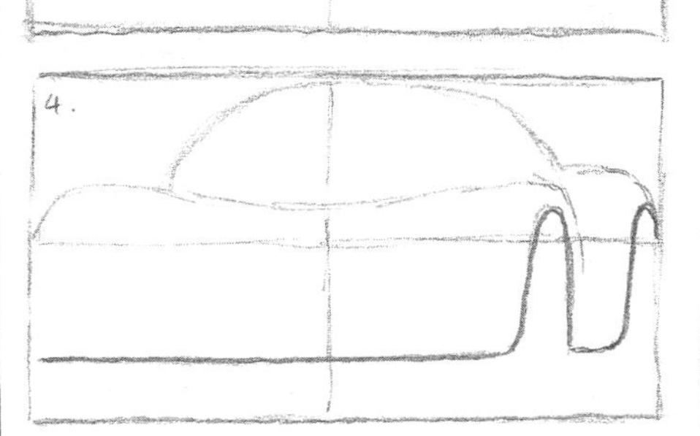

NOW SHADE WITH CROSS-HATCHING, AS IF THE LIGHT WAS COMING FROM ABOVE.

SMUDGE THE CROSS-HATCHING WITH YOUR FINGER, SMOOTHING IT ALL OUT.

FINISH OFF BY USING THE EDGE OF YOUR ERASER TO MAKE HIGHLIGHTS.

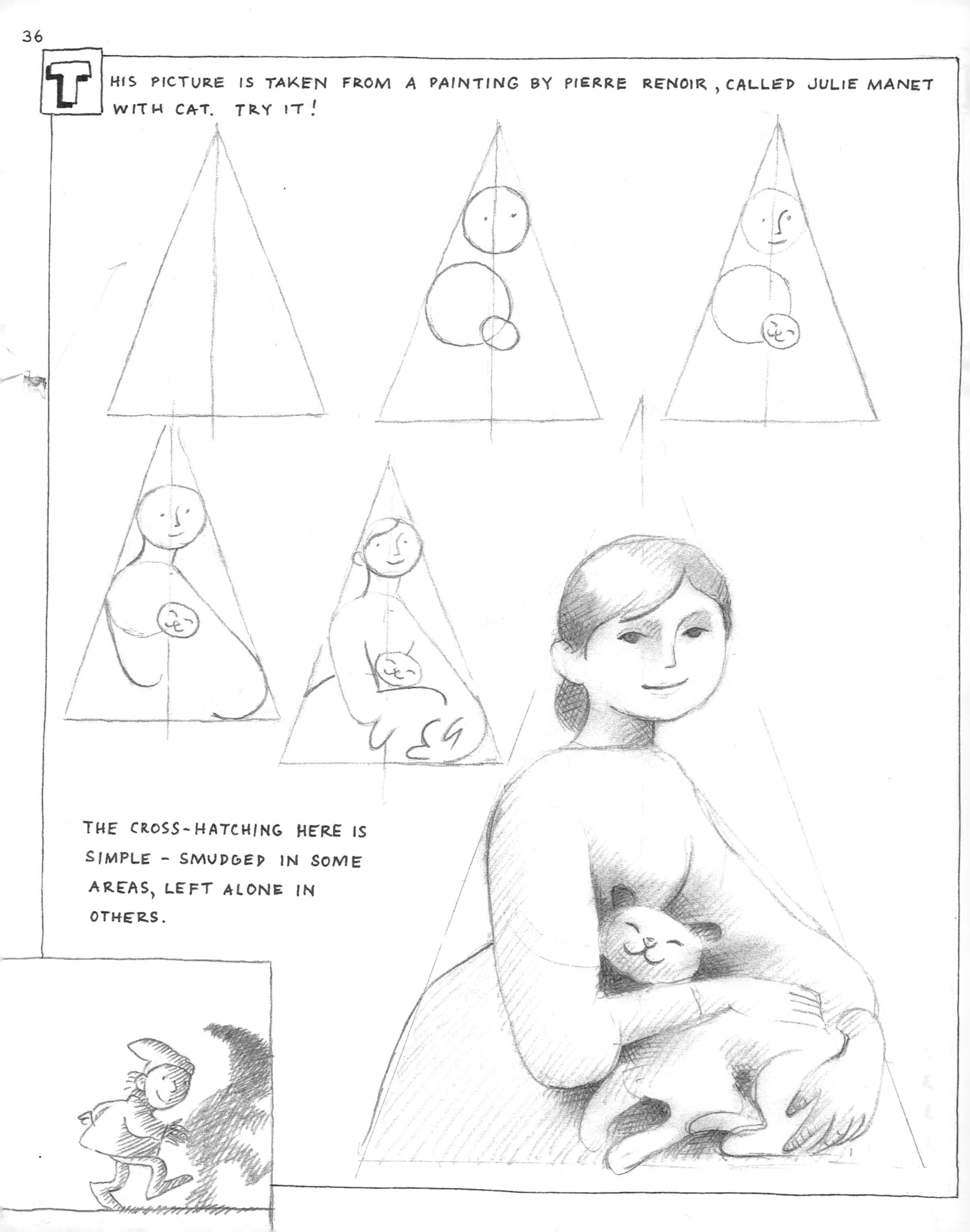
THIS PICTURE IS TAKEN FROM A PAINTING BY PIERRE RENOIR, CALLED JULIE MANET WITH CAT. TRY IT!
THE CROSS-HATCHING HERE IS SIMPLE - SMUDGED IN SOME AREAS, LEFT ALONE IN OTHERS.

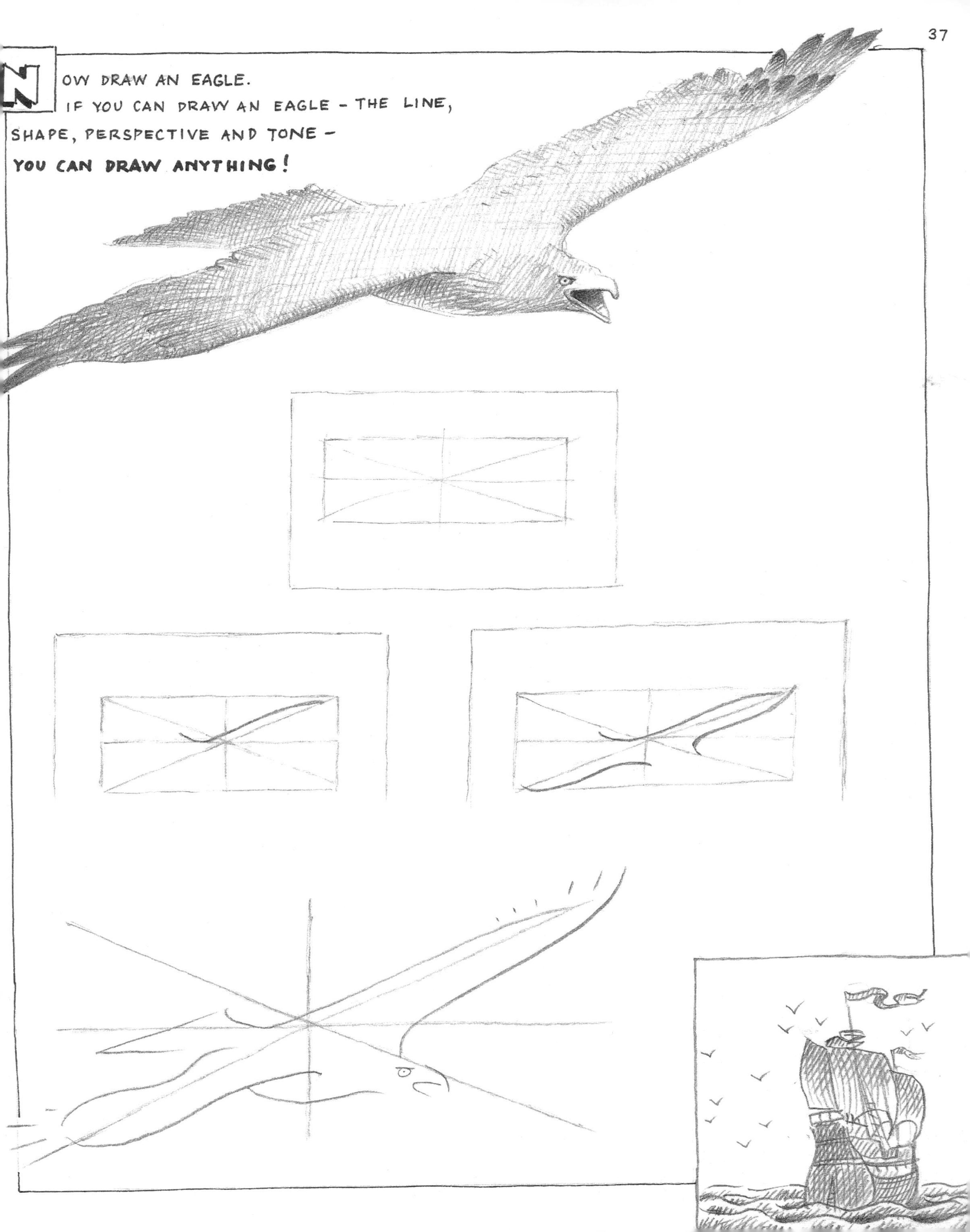
NOW DRAW AN EAGLE.
IF YOU CAN DRAW AN EAGLE - THE LINE, SHAPE, PERSPECTIVE AND TONE -
YOU CAN DRAW ANYTHING!

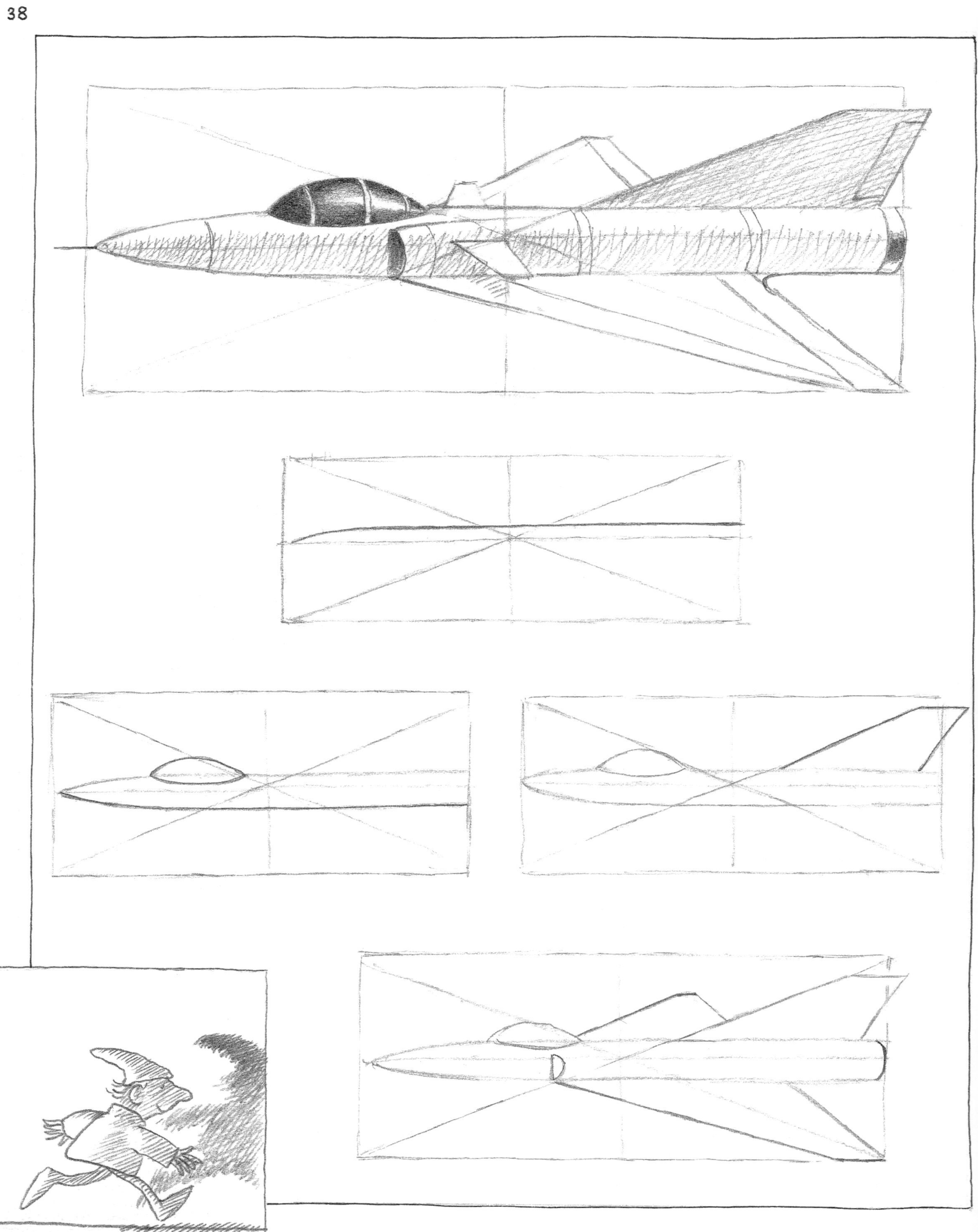